YOUR KNOWLEDGE HAS VALUE

- We will publish your bachelor's and master's thesis, essays and papers

- Your own eBook and book - sold worldwide in all relevant shops

- Earn money with each sale

Upload your text at www.GRIN.com and publish for free

Bibliographic information published by the German National Library:

The German National Library lists this publication in the National Bibliography; detailed bibliographic data are available on the Internet at http://dnb.dnb.de .

This book is copyright material and must not be copied, reproduced, transferred, distributed, leased, licensed or publicly performed or used in any way except as specifically permitted in writing by the publishers, as allowed under the terms and conditions under which it was purchased or as strictly permitted by applicable copyright law. Any unauthorized distribution or use of this text may be a direct infringement of the author s and publisher s rights and those responsible may be liable in law accordingly.

Imprint:

Copyright © 2016 GRIN Verlag, Open Publishing GmbH
Print and binding: Books on Demand GmbH, Norderstedt Germany
ISBN: 9783656988151

This book at GRIN:

http://www.grin.com/en/e-book/337114/minimizing-localization-delays-mild-for-wireless-sensor-networks

Furqan Jameel

Minimizing Localization Delays (MILD) for Wireless Sensor Networks

GRIN Publishing

GRIN - Your knowledge has value

Since its foundation in 1998, GRIN has specialized in publishing academic texts by students, college teachers and other academics as e-book and printed book. The website www.grin.com is an ideal platform for presenting term papers, final papers, scientific essays, dissertations and specialist books.

Visit us on the internet:

http://www.grin.com/

http://www.facebook.com/grincom

http://www.twitter.com/grin_com

MInimizing Localization Delays (MILD) for Wireless Sensor Networks

COMSATS Institute of Information Technology, Islamabad

Due to the success of rapidly evolving wireless sensor networks (WSN), innovating localization techniques have been proposed by researchers all over the world. Since wireless sensor nodes are small devices with limited processing power and the channel conditions are difficult to predict, therefore, there is a desperate need of a low complexity algorithm that can efficiently identify channel condition and select an appropriate method of localization. Related to this, I present in this article a novel localization scheme that is very efficient in detecting the location in real world environment which is usually a mixed case of line of sight and non-line of sight. Simulation results show that this scheme reduces the delays in localization and increases the lifetime of nodes while maintain a fairly low mean estimation error. The results also demonstrate that this scheme performs fairly well even when there are limited numbers of anchor nodes.

I. INTRODUCTION

Estimating the location of a roaming sensor node is one the most essential tasks of a wireless sensor network application. For example, if sensor nodes are deployed to provide protection against fire and each sensor node sends alarm message to other sensor nodes when it experiences sudden rise in temperature. In such a crucial situation we want to know the exact location of those sensor nodes in very short period of time, so that proper actions can be taken accordingly. Another useful example can be vehicular sensor networks. Since communicating cars and roadside infrastructure collectively form a sensor network. Therefore it is very important to know the exact location of car for collision avoidance, traffic light status information and traffic congestion information etc. Moreover, some of the promising and famous routing protocols, such as geographical routing [1, 2], make routing decisions on the basis of the location of sensor nodes. Keeping in view these facts and many more a sophisticated localization scheme is necessary i.e. a scheme which is fairly efficient even in case of very small number of anchor nodes.

The proposed scheme is a selective scheme based on the information gained through received signal strength (RSS). This scheme is divided into following major tasks:

- The unsettled node whose location is to be calculated receives broadcast messages from the anchor nodes.
- Based on the received power from these anchor nodes, the unsettled node calculates the variance of the RSS and estimates whether a particular node has line of sight with the unsettled node or not.
- After calculating the variance of all the anchor nodes it then sends this information to the sink node.
- The unsettled node selects among the two localization scheme (i.e. trilateration or multilateration) to estimate its position with sufficient accuracy.

The remainder of the paper is organized as follows. Section II discusses the lateration techniques used in this article. Next in Section III, the proposed scheme is discussed in detail with two of its subparts. In Section IV, I analytically evaluate the performance of the proposed scheme. Finally, Section V provides some concluding comments.

II. LATERATION TECHNIQUES

The optimal localization scheme that is proposed in this research paper uses two of the most well renowned RSSI-based localization techniques i.e. trilateration and multilateration

Trilateration: Trilateration is a method to obtain relative position of the point in space by measuring distance, using geometrical shapes like triangle, circles and sphere.

Since I am only considering two dimensional space therefore, only circles are considered. we need atleast three circles to estimate the position of a point in 2-D space. The interersection of these three circles will give   the estimated position of a point. This phenomenon is shown in following diagram:

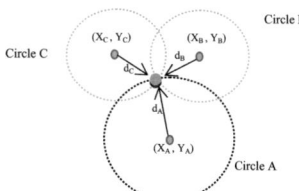

Fig. 1. Trilateration technique using three circles

The general equation of a circle is given by:

$$d^2 = x^2 + y^2 \qquad (1)$$

For a circle centered at (X_A, Y_A) the above equation can be written as:

$$d_A{}^2 = (x - x_A)^2 + (y - y_A)^2 \qquad (2)$$

Similarly for circles B and C

$$d_B{}^2 = (x - x_B)^2 + (y - y_B)^2 \qquad (3)$$

$$d_C{}^2 = (x - x_C)^2 + (y - y_C)^2 \qquad (4)$$

Equations (2.0), (3.0) and (4.0) can be expanded by opening the square:

$$d_A{}^2 = x^2 + x_A^2 - 2xx_A + y^2 + y_A^2 - 2yy_A \qquad (5)$$

$$d_B{}^2 = x^2 + x_B^2 - 2xx_B + y^2 + y_B^2 - 2yy_B \qquad (6)$$

$$d_C{}^2 = x^2 + x_C^2 - 2xx_C + y^2 + y_C^2 - 2yy_C \qquad (7)$$

In order to find the point of intersection equations (5), (6) and (7) are solved as:

$$(x^2 + y^2) - 2xx_A - 2yy_A = d_A{}^2 - x_A^2 - y_A^2 \qquad (8)$$

$$(x^2 + y^2) - 2xx_B - 2yy_B = d_B{}^2 - x_B^2 - y_B^2 \qquad (9)$$

$$(x^2 + y^2) - 2xx_C - 2yy_C = d_C{}^2 - x_C^2 - y_C^2 \qquad (10)$$

Rewriting equations (8), (9) and (10) into matrix representation, we get;

$$\begin{bmatrix} 1 & -2x_A & -2y_A \\ 1 & -2x_B & -2y_B \\ 1 & -2x_C & -2y_C \end{bmatrix} \begin{bmatrix} x^2 + y^2 \\ x \\ y \end{bmatrix} = \begin{bmatrix} d_A{}^2 - x_A^2 - y_A^2 \\ d_B{}^2 - x_B^2 - y_B^2 \\ d_C{}^2 - x_C^2 - y_C^2 \end{bmatrix} \qquad (11)$$

The above equation can also be written in following form:

3

$$A \cdot x = b \qquad (12)$$

The solution of $\hat{x}$ can be found using least square method. Hence the above equation becomes:

$$\hat{x} = (A^T . A)^{-1} A^T . b \qquad (13)$$

It is to be noted that value of matrix A and b can easily be found using only reference points and within a small fraction of time. Since it is only matrix multiplication, therefore, no extensive computation is needed.

Multilateration: It a proven localization scheme that has been used for military purposes for decades. There are many flavors of multilatertion but in this article I am only considering Nonlinear Least Square Multilateration. It is a variation of Newton method for finding a smallest of a function. It uses Gauss-Newton method to find the minimum value of a function. Initially, the position of a node is randomly selected, let this random position be (X_r, Y_r). Moreover, equation (11) can be written in general form as:

$$\begin{bmatrix} 1 & -2x_A & -2y_A \\ 1 & -2x_B & -2y_B \\ : & : & : \\ 1 & -2x_N & -2y_N \end{bmatrix} \begin{bmatrix} x^2 + y^2 \\ x \\ y \end{bmatrix} = \begin{bmatrix} d_A{}^2 - x_A^2 - y_A^2 \\ d_B{}^2 - x_B^2 - y_B^2 \\ : \\ d_N{}^2 - x_N^2 - y_N^2 \end{bmatrix}$$

Where N represents the total number of nodes which is greater than three. The equation (13) can be rewritten as delta:

$$\Delta_N = (A_N^T . A_N)^{-1} A_N^T . b$$

$$(X_i, Y_i) = (X_r, Y_r) - \Delta_i$$

Where Δ_i represents the delta value of ith node whose location is represented by (X_i, Y_i). Iterative method is used to accurately locate the position of a node. As the number of iterations increase the estimated location of (X_i, Y_i) becomes more precise as shown in figure below. As the area increases the number of iterations to correctly estimate the location of node must also be increased. Furthermore, with the increase in number of anchor nodes the value of delta reduces for same area. This shows that as the no. of anchor nodes increases the value of delta also reduces. Hence, less number of iterations is required for estimating the position of sensor node correctly.

4

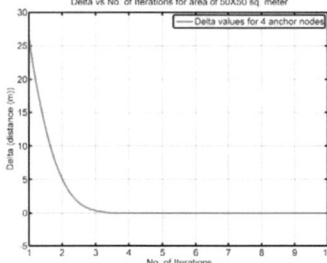

Fig. 2. Delta value vs iterations for area of 50 sq. meters

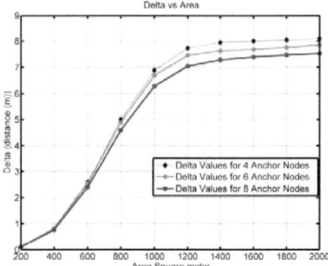

Fig. 3. Increase in Delta value with the increase in area for specific number of anchor nodes

Dependence on RSSI:

The above mentioned techniques will give accurate position of x and y i.e. the position of the required node. Since these techniques depend heavily on measured distance and due to the complexity of modeling the environmental effects the RSS-based distances are not always correct. Therefore, many physical phenomenons like scattering, diffraction and reflection cause diverse path losses for same distances.

Measurements have confirmed that at any given distance the path loss is random and follows a normal distribution. Hence the probability distribution of estimated distance is given by:

$$10nlog\left(\frac{\hat{d}}{d_0}\right) - 10nlog\left(\frac{d}{d_0}\right) = X_\sigma\,[dB] \qquad (14)$$

The above equation can also be written as:

$$\hat{d} = d + d(10^{\frac{X_\sigma}{10n}} - 1) \qquad (15)$$

Where X_σ is Gaussian random variable with zero mean and standard deviation σ, n is the path loss coefficient, d is the actual distance and $\hat{d}$ is the measured distance.

This standard deviation increases in case of Non-Line of Sight (i.e. the variation of channel increases) which will effect on the overall measure distance. This will resultantly increase the error in estimation of position of unsettled node.

5

III. PROBLEM SETUP

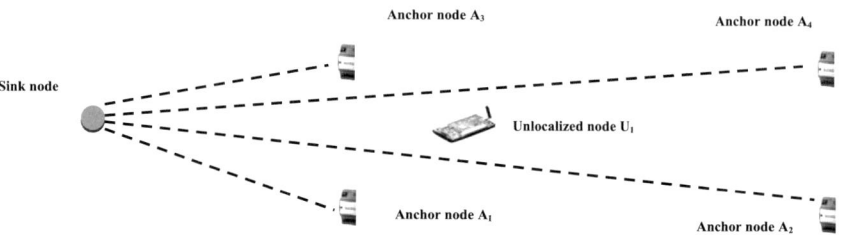

Anchor node A₃

Anchor node A₄

Sink node

Unlocalized node U₁

Anchor node A₁

Anchor node A₂

Fig. 4. Problem setup containing a sink node, four anchor nodes and an unsettled sensor node

As shown in Fig. 1, I consider wireless sensor network consisting of a sink node and five sensor nodes. Out of these sensor nodes four are anchor nodes A1 , A2 , A3 and A4 whereas, there is one un-localized nodes U1. I have assumed that all the anchor nodes know their position through GPS receiver. The coordinates of anchor nodes are (X_k, Y_k), where k=1,2,3,4. The anchor nodes transmit the information about their location with a signal of normalized intensity to an un-localized node U1. Sink node has the connectivity to the entire network. It is also considered that channel is quasi-static between sink node and anchor node (i.e. it does not vary for a given transmission time). In this problem only the energy dissipated by unsettled node is considered, since in most of the real world scenarios unsettled node is the one with limited amount of energy. Sink node is able to transmit and receive data to every single node in the network. However, it has only information about the location of the anchor nodes and it does not know the location of U_1 in the network.

Proposed Scheme:

1. Channel Prediction:

Whenever the sink node wants to find the location of an unsettled node, it first asks all the anchor nodes to be in transmission mode and unsettled node to be in reception mode. The mobile node receives the signal strength from all the anchor nodes. The unsettled node receives the pulse input through an unknown channel. It then analyses the variance of RSS. Based on the experimentally determined value of threshold it decides whether the channel is line of sight or non-line of sight. For both line of sight and non-line of sight channel the variance is shown in the following diagrams:

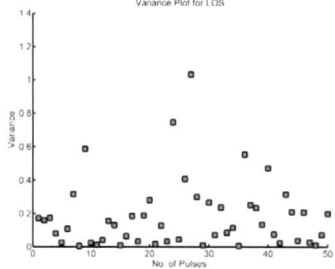

6

Fig. 5. Variance value for line of sight environment

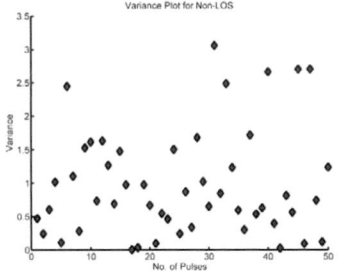

Fig. 6. Variance value for non-line of sight environment

The value of threshold that determines whether channel is LOS or NLOS with around 80% accuracy can easily be determined from following graph:

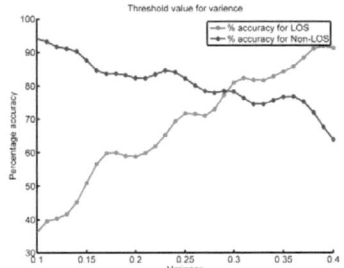

Fig. 7. Determination of threshold value to differentiate between line of sight and non-line of sight environment

Hence the condition of the channel can be found from given relationship:

$\sigma_{calculated} < \sigma_{thr}$:LOS channel

$\sigma_{calculated} > \sigma_{thr}$:NLOS channel

Where $\sigma_{calculated}$ is the calculated value of variance for a given set of pulses, σ_{thr} is the experimentally determined value of threshold of variance i.e. 0.3. This process is done for RSS value of all the anchor nodes. Since this process does not involve any sort of complex computation, therefore, the delay caused by this process is negligible and does not significantly affect the overall delay.

2. *Localization*
a. *Case 1: when 3 or more nodes have LOS*

When unsettled node has line of sight with three or more nodes it shows that the distance calculation that will be done for localization would not be affected much. Furthermore, the variance of the noise added in case of line of sight will not be great enough to cause any serious problems in localization. This condition favors the use of trilateration technique. Hence the unsettled node uses trilateration method for

7

localization to estimate its position and informs the sink node regarding its co-ordinates. Since trilateration method involves only multiplication of matrix in a linear fashion, therefore, this localization technique is suitable for unsettled node and will not increase the complexity of hardware of sensor node.

b. Case 2: when less than 3 nodes have LOS

When unsettled node has line of sight with less than three anchor nodes it shows that channel conditions are not suitable to use trilateration technique. Since the distance calculation from non-line of sight anchor nodes will inculcate high variation of added noise. Using trilateration with further worsen the location estimation as trilateration itself uses linear method to calculate position of node. It leads us to multilateration. However, multilateration due to its non-linear computation method is not a good choice for sensor node, as it will increase the complexity of hardware and will require more computation power. Therefore, the sensor node will inform about the situation to sink node. The sink node will then send a command to unsettled node to change to transmission mode and will also inform anchor nodes to change to reception mode. The unsettled node will then send 1000 bit pulse to all the anchor nodes at least 5 times (since at least 5 iterations are required to make the value of delta zero for area of 100 sq. meter and correctly estimate position). The anchor nodes will receives these pulses and calculate the distance individually and will send these distances to sink node. The sink node will then use the multilateration technique to calculate the co-ordinates of unsettled node.

IV. PERFORMANCE EVALUATION

1. Delay Reduction:

It is vividly clear from the following diagrams that the localization delay has been significantly reduced. Even when the number of sensor nodes increase significantly. These graphs have been drawn for 4 anchor nodes which show that the proposed scheme performs fairly well even with limited number of anchor nodes.

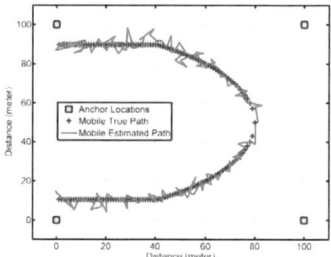

Fig. 7. Estimated path of mobile sensor node using the proposed scheme

There is up to 1 meter mean estimation error which is insignificant as compare to the area ($100m^2$). Moreover, the proposed scheme successfully detects the mobility pattern of the sensor node which is extremely helpful in navigation. In case of multilateration the delay curve increases very rapidly, whereas, for the proposed scheme delay curve increases at a slow pace; even for large number of sensor node. The results show that the proposed scheme's mean estimation error is at par with multilateration used in LOS environment, even when the proposed scheme experiences mixed (LOS and NLOS) environment.

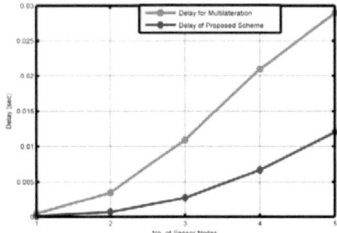

Fig. 8. Delay comparison of multilateration technique and proposed scheme using 4 anchor nodes

2. Energy Consumption:

The energy models for a wireless sensor node use an elementary assumption that a sensor node consumes it power in three functions: communication (energy transmission and energy reception), processing the data and acquisition.

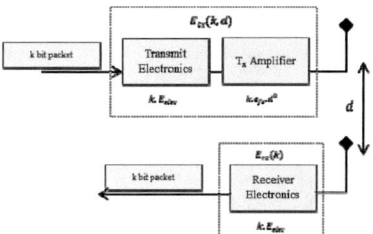

Fig. 9. Energy consumption model

The first function i.e. communication consumes a large amount of power due to the fact that it constitutes of two sub-operations. The energy model used in this article is called the first-order radio model. According this model, the node consumes $E_{tx}(k,d)$ amount of energy in transmitting p bits of information over a distance given by d [4].

$$E_{tx}(k,d) = k.E_{elec} + k.\varepsilon_{fs}.d^\alpha \qquad (16)$$

When k bits of information is transmitted by N nodes the total energy is given by:

$$Energy_N = k.\{\textstyle\sum_{i=1}^{N}(E_{elec} + \varepsilon_{fs}.d_i^\alpha)\} \qquad (17)$$

Whereas, $E_{rx}(k)$ is amount of energy that is consumed when p bits of information are received, given by:

$$E_{rx}(k) = k.E_{elec} \qquad (18)$$

9

Parameter	Definition	Units
E_{elec}	Energy dissipation rate to run the radio	50nJ/bit
α	Path loss coefficient	2.5
ε_{fs}	One path model for the transmitter amplifier	10pJ/bitm^2
k	Data length	1000 bits

Table 1. Definition of parameters used in energy consumption model [4]

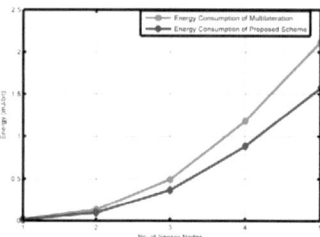

Fig. 10. Energy consumption comparison of multilateration technique and proposed scheme using 4 anchor nodes

The simulation result show that the proposed scheme performs better than the multilateration scheme. It is to be noted that the difference between energy consumption, as compare to the multilatertion, increases when the number of sensor nodes increase. This difference is due to the fact that as the numbers of sensor nodes increase the probability of finding line of sight with anchor nodes increase. This results into utilization of trilateration technique, which operates in reception mode, hence utilizing less power.

V. CONCLUSION AND FUTURE RESEARCH

In this article I have proposed a scheme that focuses on reduction of delay during localization at the same time utilizing minimum amount of energy. It is done while maintain a fairly low position estimation error. It shows that the proposed scheme is extremely useful for detecting the position of highly mobile (i.e. delay intolerant) wireless sensor nodes. This article also introduces a simple yet effective mechanism to detect the channel condition in case of both LOS and NLOS.

In this paper, I only examined the delays and energy consumption for single antenna, where each anchor and sensor node is equipped with only one antenna for transmission and reception. However, it is of high interest to extend the results of delay and energy consumption for a MIMO system utilizing multiple antennas. Keeping in view that for channel condition multiple or single antenna can be used which can lead to fascinating possibilities. I leave this thought-provoking and interesting problem for future work.

VI. REFERENCES

[1] Karp, B., Kung, H.T.: GPSR: Greedy perimeter stateless routing for wireless networks. In: Proc. Of the Int. Conf. on Mobile Computing and Networking (MOBICOM), pp. 243–254 (2000)

[2] Yu, Y., Govindan, R., Estrin, D.: Geographical and energy aware routing: A recursive data dissemination protocol for wireless sensor networks. Technical Report UCLA/CSD-TR-01-0023, UCLA Computer Science Department (2001)

[3] Dixon, John C., (2009), "Suspension Analysis and computational Geometry: John Wiley and sons limited

[4] J. Wang and Y. K. Lee, "Determination of the optimal Hop number for wireless sensor networks," in Proceedings of the International Conference on Computational Science and Its Applications: Part II,Seoul,Korea,2009.

[5] A. Pages-Zamora, J. Vidal, and D.H. Brooks, "Closed-form solution for positioning based on angle of arrival measurements", The 13th IEEE Int. Symposium Personal, Indoor and Mobile Radio Communications, vol. 4, Sep 2002.

[6] S. Capkum, M. Hamdi and J.P Hubaux, (2004), "GPS- free positioning in mobile ad-hoc networks". In Hawaii international conference in system sciences (Hicss -34), pages 3481-3490, maul, Hawaii

[7] B. Han, D. Z. Zhang and T. Yang, "Energy Consumption Analysis and Energy Management Strategy for Sensor Node," International Conference on Information and Automation, Proceedings of the 2008 IEEE, Vol. 6, 2008, pp. 211-214.

YOUR KNOWLEDGE HAS VALUE

- We will publish your bachelor's and
  master's thesis, essays and papers

- Your own eBook and book -
  sold worldwide in all relevant shops

- Earn money with each sale

Upload your text at www.GRIN.com
and publish for free